Dating Tips for Women

21 Dating Tips and Dating Advice for Women to Get the Guy and Keep Him

by Chase Scott

Table of Contents

Introduction 1

Key Tip #1 7

Key Tip #2 11

Key Tip #3 13

Key Tip #4 15

Key Tip #5 17

Key Tip #6 19

Key Tip #7 21

Key Tip #8 25

Key Tip #9 29

Key Tip #10 31

Key Tip #11 33

Key Tip #12 37

Key Tip #13 39

Key Tip #14 43

Key Tip #15 47

Key Tip #16 53

Key Tip #17 57

Key Tip #18 61

Key Tip #19 65

Key Tip #20 69

Key Tip #21 73

Conclusion 79

Introduction

Dating can sometimes feel like a battle ground, where two people show up but only one, or maybe even none, walks away unscarred. But does it really have to be so taxing? Do we do it to ourselves? And what elementary, easily avoidable mistakes do we make that result in relationships so twisted that they would put Pilates-practicing-pretzels to shame?

I once heard from an older couple that "a dream partner isn't just someone who you love and who loves you, or even someone you fit perfectly with, but somebody that you want to continue to **grow** with for the rest of your life, damn the ups and downs." The fact that they were in their late-60s, had been together since their mid-20s, and still looked at each other with sickeningly cute puppy-love in their eyes, tended to lend their advice some gravitas.

Nothing makes more sense than a good relationship, and yet somehow nothing is more confusing than trying to get in, and stay in, one. Dating is fun, but if you want to be truly happy then you need to listen to your heart as well as your head, and find someone who can, to a certain extent, satisfy both. There is no such thing as a perfect partner, just a devoted one, ready to work through anything by your side. You have to be the same to them.

As you read this book, pay attention especially to the points that resonate with you most, making you rethink, or consider changing even a single aspect of your approach to dating. By devoting yourself to implementing a few of these changes, you will find that your relationships become instantly easier, smoother, and more enjoyable.

Before we get started, here are three critical edicts that we are hopefully already on the same page about:

1. Dating is <u>Not</u> a status symbol.

2. Who you d<u>ate</u> says absolutely <u>nothing</u> about you. You are defined by yourself – your own values, beliefs, and actions – not by who you have on your arm.

3. There is no such thing as an easy relationship, just one that's easy to start. This is especially true of any relationship truly worth having. Whether or not you're willing to work on it is what sets apart a worthy relationship vs. the alternative.

So, with those out of the way, let's move on to the key tips for dating success that might help you find –

and keep – that relationship you've been craving!

© Copyright 2014 by LCPublifish LLC - All rights reserved.

This document is geared towards providing reliable information in regard to the topic and issue covered. The publication is sold with the idea that the publisher is not required to render accounting, officially permitted, or otherwise, qualified services. If advice is necessary, legal or professional, a practiced individual in the profession should be ordered.

- From a Declaration of Principles which was accepted and approved equally by a Committee of the American Bar Association and a Committee of Publishers and Associations.

In no way is it legal to reproduce, duplicate, or transmit any part of this document in either electronic means or in printed format. Recording of this publication is strictly prohibited and any storage of this document is not allowed unless with written permission from the publisher. All rights reserved.

The information provided herein is stated to be truthful and consistent, in that any liability, in terms of inattention or otherwise, by any usage or abuse of any policies, processes, or directions contained within is solely and completely the responsibility of the recipient reader. Under no circumstances will any legal responsibility or blame be held against the publisher for any reparation, damages, or monetary loss due to the information herein, either directly or indirectly.

Respective authors own all copyrights not held by the publisher.

The information herein is offered for informational purposes solely, and is universal as so. The presentation of the information is without contract or any type of guarantee assurance.

The trademarks that are used are without any consent, and the publication of the trademark is without permission or backing by the trademark owner. All trademarks and brands within this book are for clarifying purposes only and are the owned by the owners themselves, not affiliated with this document.

Key Tip #1

Love Thyself

As cliché as it might sound, this is a very important tip. Having self-confidence, knowing what you love about yourself and what value you can bring, is a key part of being the right person in any relationship. Why would someone else find you worthy of loving, when you don't even love yourself? Know who you are first, and accept that it's okay to have sides of you which you wish were different. You don't have to be the "perfect version of yourself" from day one, as long as you know which direction you want to head to get there.

The confidence that comes from accepting who you are is also a definite positive, since confidence is *always* attractive. It won't happen in a day, but it will never happen if you never start. Besides, if someone needs you to change drastically, then they are probably not the right person for you anyway.

There are plenty of ways to increase your love for yourself. One of the best starting points is to make a list of all the good things about yourself, including everything ranging from random physical attributes ("I have nice fingernails") to skills ("My tennis forehand is unstoppable", "I am pretty good at drawing and painting") to education or professional abilities ("I have a Masters degree from a good college" or "I'm efficient and effective at my job") to your support system ("I have a sweet mother who would do anything for me", "I have a strong network of wonderful friends") to quirks ("I'm goofy and fun when I feel comfortable around somebody") to other internal beliefs and values ("I speak honestly and act with integrity"). The list should be long – and if it isn't, then you're not trying hard enough. If you need help, ask some of your closest friends what they like about you as a starting point. But then always try to see these things in yourself.

Key Tip #2

Feeling Desperate? Take a Break!

If you feel like you're starting to become desperate to be with someone, or anyone, now is the perfect time to take a break and devote some time to yourself. Desperation, as a trait, is about as subtle as Thor, standing in the middle of Times Square, wearing a neon green thong Speedo swimsuit. Not only is it a turn-off for quality partners, it leaves you wide open to sleazebags.

It's not just an accident or myth that most great couples find each other when they least expect it. Instead of obsessively trying to squeeze dates out of venues where there are none worth having, just concentrate on getting out of your house and living, just for the fun of it! Spend more time doing new and interesting things with your friends or by yourself. Expand your horizons. There's definitely a lot more to living life than aimlessly dating, if you only give yourself a chance to explore.

Key Tip #3

Know What You Want (Experiment While Dating, But Not Aimlessly)

It's always fun to have plenty of dating options, and to date different kinds of people. Even still, if you're not sure of the kind of people you like, or who would mesh well with you, then you will have almost no control over your dating life.

I'm not saying that you shouldn't try to date different kinds of people, but if you've realized that a certain type just doesn't work well with you, try and avoid the pattern. Easier said than done, I know, but this is where you must use your intellect and instinct to your advantage.

Try refining your image of an ideal mate through each interaction you have, and then look for someone who has those sets of qualities which you **know** work well with you. It's time to stop day-dreaming about 'Prince Charming', who usually turns out to be emotional toads, warts and all. Thinking about what you want will save you a lot of unnecessary heart-ache.

Key Tip #4

Stick to Your Own Priorities (Be Scrutinizing)

Having a clear idea of your priorities lets you steer yourself towards the kind of relationship that would best fulfill your needs and desires, whether for the short-term or long. This is true whether you're just looking to have fun with someone, experiencing some companionship and intimacy in your preciously rare free-time, or whether you're looking for someone to have a long-term devoted relationship with. You can only find someone whose life vision matches yours if you know your own in the first place. While these priorities and needs may change from time to time, you should at least have a clear idea of your needs of the moment.

Key Tip #5

First and Foremost, Have Fun

Once you meet someone you like, don't get busy rushing into things (namely, bed). First, get to know the other person and see if you can just have fun in each other's company, without the need for alcohol or sex.

Fun and smiles are under-rated, and dating isn't a transaction between accountants. What do you think it says about the likelihood of forming a real bond, if you can't even have fun in your partner's company? Not likely.

Key Tip #6

Texts Only? Give Him the Boot!

If someone's only communicating with you via text, your best advice is to kick him out of your life and move on; regardless of the reasons he may use to justify it. Something's either supremely shady about the situation, or he's treating you with gross disrespect and you deserve better.

This tip holds irrespective of their personal situation, and however recently you may have met and started dating. If they don't think you're worthy of even short phone calls or face-to-face meetings, whether physically or via web-cams and video chats, you're obviously far too low on their list of priorities. Worse, they may simply be treating you like a booty-call. In this case they aren't worthy of your time and attention either.

Key Tip #7

Don't Undersell Yourself

Sometimes we're so concerned with wanting to seem modest, or not wanting to brag, that we severely undersell ourselves. This tends to backfire because it gets in the way of a prospective partner getting to know the 'real you' better, and can make you seem dull.

It may be that you just aren't comfortable talking about yourself too freely, or you're a little too shy to bring up your own achievements or skills, or are worried about intimidating the other person. In this case, a good rule of thumb may be to wait for your date to bring up a question or line of conversation that would be relevant to your experiences, rather than trying to bring up the topic yourself. It's also worth considering that a date who isn't mature enough to handle your achievements may not be the kind of person you want to spend time with.

However, some great partners do have this issue. A good solution if you still want them in your life is to show them that you rely on them in other ways. Let them do small tasks for you, even if you would've been able to do them yourself, and make them feel appreciated for it. This helps you to manage this issue, makes them feel needed, and keeps an otherwise great dating experience on track.

It may be that the situation is reversed, and you feel intimidated or daunted by your partner and his achievements or abilities. In this case, the mistake that most people naturally make is to try and drag the other person down to their comfort zone, to limit the other so as to feel better about themselves. If you feel this way, understand and accept that you need to grow, but that the other person likes you and enjoys your company all the same. Try and push through your limits – match theirs, instead of the other way around. Isn't that how you would want your partner to act? By ensuring that neither of you are underselling yourselves or feeling intimidated, you can both grow together productively, instead of limiting yourselves through one person's hang-ups.

Key Tip #8

But Don't Oversell Either

Perhaps the more common situation that we face when meeting someone we like is an urge to oversell or magnify certain aspects of who we are. Whether it's a personality trait that we think they may like more, or exaggerated achievements and skills, most people indulge in it regularly when meeting dates for the first time. So, you're definitely not alone.

The thing to keep in mind here is the line between a harmless exaggeration and a bold-faced lie. Try to think it through. Even if you lie at this point to make yourself more likeable, your partner will eventually uncover the truth. Do you really want thoughts like, "She lied to me about how good she was at Ping Pong when we met. I wonder what else she lied about. Do I really know this girl? Can I trust her?" going through the other person's mind? Would you want them going through yours, especially for a lie that your date could have easily avoided? Keep exaggerations to a minimum, and stay away from lies. They'll come back to haunt you, and by that point, fixing them will be too little too late.

If you're ever tempted to lie about yourself, think

about this quote – "Whoever is careless with the truth in small matters cannot be trusted with important matters." - Albert Einstein. It's something that a lot of people could do with remembering.

Key Tip #9

Common Interests vs. Common Values

It's easy to confuse these two important traits when searching for a suitable partner, and it's a mistake that many make. More often than not, it leads to questions like 'We like the same things, so why do we always fight?', or 'We want the same things out of life, so why don't we like spending time with each other?'

Relationships are always about give and take, along a common path. If you don't have any common interests, it leaves you without shared passions to talk about. If you don't have common values, then you don't see your lives heading in the same direction. Keep this in mind while dating, since having both of these things is the first step to a happy relationship.

While both factors can be worked on by caring partners, it's important to understand and accept your differences in order to take the next step forward. If you feel like either one of these two areas is missing in your relationship, talk to your partner about how you can work it through. Finding overlapping beliefs and objectives about the kind of work-place, friends or family you each want to be a part of usually helps to find common values.

Key Tip #10

Best Friends Over Best Looks

The best dating experiences, and the relationships that seamlessly follow, are based equally on chemistry, concern, and effort. Without exception, the relationships that last are those where the people involved don't just want to tear each other's clothes off, but also want to spend time as best friends afterwards.

You need to check that your current dating criteria will allow you to meet someone who can give you all that. If it doesn't, then maybe it's time for some internal reflection. Though there's nothing wrong with wanting to be with a good-looking partner, if external appearances are your largest priority then you're really killing your chances of finding success and long-lasting happiness.

Key Tip #11

Friends with Benefits (the Myth!)

Most people look at the concept of "friends with benefits" as a god-send, a magical lala-land of sorts. They think they somehow defy the laws of relationships and all the responsibilities and complications that come with them, while providing fun with a friend who you get along with and enjoy spending time with anyway. Sure, and while you're at it, let's just say that stilettos are easy to walk in, pencil skirts are as comfortable as sweat pants, and lipstick actually lasts all day long.

I charge my laptop's battery on Pokémon power, ride to work on the Loch Ness monster, and get a back-massage from a Yeti every evening.

Here's the inconvenient truth, this magical loophole that everyone seems to think exists is nothing but a myth. It's usually either two people who have enough emotions between them to start a relationship but are both wimping out, or an easy booty-call for one or the other. It rarely works out for both partners, at least after a while anyway.

Either way it's just another quick-fix to avoid facing a

situation – to stay in a bubble because it's so warm and cozy in there. But, yet again, what do you think will happen once that bubble bursts? All that's left is the confusion, pain and complications of a relationship, with all the heart-ache of one when it ends, without having even had a proper one in the first place.

My advice about friends with benefits is simple – stay away from it. Even if you both tell each other that neither will complicate matters, sooner or later one of you will develop strong emotions and want more. It's really unavoidable.

If both of you want to be together badly enough to resort to this poor excuse for an arrangement, just hold back from defining yourselves as anything more till some time passes, and start dating properly in the meanwhile. When it comes to dating, the easier-looking path is usually the one that's the messiest to clean up afterwards.

Key Tip #12

Sure, 'Opposites Attract', But You'll Need More Later

While the chemistry and attraction that comes from the 'Opposites Attract' effect may often be fun, what do you think will happen once that novelty wears off? Intense chemistry serves as a good base to build a lasting partnership, in fact sometimes, the stronger the better. But if that's the one thing that you keep relying on, then the relationship is doomed to be short-lived.

You need to start working with your partner to find common ground. Since complete polar opposites are an utter rarity, you may find common interests that you already share but didn't know, or new passions and hobbies that neither of you have tried before but which you may both turn out to be quite interested in pursuing.

Key Tip #13

Understand Your Boundaries

Everyone has their own sense of physical and emotional space, and a pace at which they're comfortable letting other people in. The toys of our digital age have definitely made the world a much smaller place, and one in which it's significantly easier to keep lines of communication open 24x7. However, it has also made us all that much more guarded about our own space and boundaries. And that's okay.

There's nothing wrong with having boundaries when you meet someone, and letting others earn their way closer to you. However, this only works as long as you don't reach a point where you're not letting people closer, regardless of their actions, because of your own issues or past emotional baggage.

If certain times of the day are not convenient for you, be clear about them from the beginning. Any boundary issues of which you are aware should be communicated from the start. Mention your boundaries, whether physical, emotional or otherwise, and if they happen to change in the future, communicate the changes too. Take care to remember that you may be on the receiving end of this as well, and be patient with your partner, instead of trying to force your way in. Remember, an inch of space earned is worth a lot more than a mile conquered.

A woman who knows her boundaries will come across as knowing what she wants, and this will earn you respect from any quality partner, as long as you don't use this as an excuse to remain indefinitely distant.

Key Tip #14

But Don't Let Boundaries Rule You

As I discussed in the section above, boundaries aren't a bad thing, but it is equally important not to let them rule you. Everyone has a comfort zone, and by and large most people don't like to venture too far outside them. So just as your boundaries and your comfort zone are important to you, and good for you to discuss with a potential partner, it's equally important not to close yourself off to new experiences. The happiest lives come with an open mind. Don't decide you don't like something without at least trying it once. After you've tried something, your opinion is based on fact and experience, not conjecture or stubbornness. No quality partner would ask more of you than a simple attempt at an experience, just as you wouldn't want any more from them than an effort at attempting something you like.

Remember that growth only comes from exposure to new experiences, thoughts and emotions. If we don't grow, then we mentally stagnate and suffocate quite fast.

Whether you're 16 or 66, you haven't done and seen everything, especially if you're the former (as much as we would all have disagreed when we were at that age). Mentally and emotionally, you'll keep growing until the day you die. So, don't let your boundaries and your comfort zone rule you and your dating life.

Even after you've been dating for a while, or are in a relationship, take care to give each other some space every day so you can continue growing as individuals. The strongest relationships aren't just the ones that grow together as a couple, but the ones where both individuals grow stronger side-by-side over time, with both their needs and desires met.

Whether the presence or absence of personal space bothers two people can only be decided together. But if you two stop growing as individuals, and lose your own identity in the bliss of togetherness, eventually it will either lead to boredom, bitterness or stagnation.

Key Tip #15

Don't Define the Relationship Too Fast, but Don't Dawdle Either

This is one of the biggest concerns for people in their dating lives. 'When do we stop 'dating', and define ourselves as something more? When's the best time to bring up the subject and how do I talk about this?'

My advice on this is that you shouldn't be in too much of a rush to define your growing bond. Enjoy yourselves and first figure out if you are both truly compatible for 'something more'. Even still, I would put the cap on this undefined bond at something around three months.

Being in a rush to define yourselves, more often than not, leads to one or the other person alienating themselves. Emotional baggage, trust and commitment issues, long-term and short-term needs, etc. all play a part in whether a couple takes the next step or not. In an ideal situation, both people involved would instinctively know and sense when the right time to move to the next level is. This would usually be within the first few weeks or months, and there would be no need for fear of awkward conversations (I wish, right?). Realistically, this seldom happens. One of the two typically reaches the stage, where they want something more, faster than the other.

If you're facing this situation, and wondering when the perfect time to bring this topic up would be, there is none. But, before you rush to broach this topic with your partner, at least ask yourselves the following questions.

- 'Does my partner care about me and my needs sufficiently for me to rely on them in the long-term?'

- 'Can I see myself with this person in the near and distant future?' (this is not necessarily up until marriage, though that should be an integral part, but at least in a happy, long-term, committed relationship)

- 'Do I feel strongly enough for this person to devote myself to them in a committed, long-term relationship, or am I just trying to settle because I don't want to be alone?'

Only if the answers to these questions point in favor of you being emotionally and mentally ready, without any deception or denial, should you worry about the next step. If you don't get any signs that your prospective partner isn't ready to talk about the next step, your next move should be to reflect on everything you know about them.

- What are their emotional issues?

- What sort of complications may be standing in their way that may prevent them committing to you?

- Do they understand your depth of concern and care for them, and are they emotionally and mentally mature enough to handle a long-term relationship?

None of the answers from these questions should stop you from talking to them, since you're basically assuming what their answers would be, without asking them. But these should help you to form a more realistic expectation of the kind of response you may get from them when you do talk to them about it.

Always remember that they may pleasantly surprise you with their response as well, because it's impossible to truly predict what another person may be thinking or feeling. Never be so afraid that you don't communicate at all. Be confident in where you stand and what you want, and prepare to express this in a way that's respectful to whatever response the other person may have.

If you've met recently, and are still in the process of getting to know each other, and if what you know of your partner doesn't give you the most optimistic answers, then my suggestion is to wait a bit longer.

In the meantime, since you already know what you want, start changing your behavior towards them slowly. Try showing them the emotional advantages of being in a relationship with you. Bring out the skills that you believe you bring to this relationship, and give them previews of what it would be like to have you as a caring, committed partner. Instead of saying the words that you may want to, perform the actions instead. For example, if you're a good cook, try cooking their favorite dishes more often, etc. Show your emotions in your behavior, touches, looks and body language. Take care to do this slowly so as to not scare them off, if they don't seem mature enough to handle these changes all at once.

But as I mentioned before, I would recommend a maximum waiting period of around three months from when you start dating. That's enough time for you to get to know each other pretty well, figure out if you two have good chemistry, if you care about each other, and if you want to be together longer exclusively or not. Don't dawdle or procrastinate beyond this time, finish the conversation so that you can at least finally know, and not drive yourself crazy thinking about the possibilities.

If they seem to need more time, then it may be safer to assume that your needs and their needs, at least for the moment, don't match.

Key Tip #16

When Is the Right Time to Say, 'I Love You'?

As discussed within the previous tip above, there is no way for one person to determine the perfect time to say it, regardless of what sitcoms and movies teach us. But if you strongly believe that it's too soon, or that your partner may not be emotionally prepared for words so momentous, then there are other ways for you to lead up to it. The basic lesson here is to reveal your emotions slowly, lightly, and casually, instead of turning it into big affairs or 'heavy' moments.

If you feel like you're ready to say, 'I love you', but your partner may not be, say 'I like you' more often. Appreciate the efforts that they put in for your happiness more often and more vocally. As with the previous section, start to display your emotions in your looks, touches and behavior more than the actual words. It's sad that there are plenty of great partners who are often scared of the words, even though they feel the same way. It might be silly, but it's still true, and you need to deal with it patiently, especially if you're sure of your feelings and that person's place in your life.

And if you do reach out and say those words first, do

it with confidence and patience. Don't expect your partner to immediately return the favor, and be prepared to wait days, weeks, or even months for him to say it back to you, especially if you are fairly certain he feels the same way based on his actions and other displays of affection. But wait with confidence instead of with fear and insecurity. Hold your head high knowing that you were maturely able to express your feelings, and knowing that you're worth loving too.

Key Tip #17

Communicate, Communicate, Communicate!

I'm going to repeat this as many times as it takes for you to remember it, Communication is vital!

This may sound cheesy, but a relationship between two people is like a canoe – if neither of you has any idea which direction the other is headed and what strokes you have to make to stay in sync, you'll soon be exhausted from paddling in opposite directions, and resentful that the other person isn't paddling with you.

Communicate your thoughts, feelings, ideas and inspirations as often as you can with your partner. It gives them a much better sense of who you are than all the spiel that was fed back and forth when you started dating. If your partner seems not to communicate as much, calmly and pleasantly ask specific questions about their day, surroundings, work, hobbies, friends, family, etc. instead of making vague statements like 'Talk to me' or worse 'Why don't you talk to me?'.

If something displeases or upsets you, don't play

games, sulk, pout, or stomp around. Just go talk to your partner face-to-face, with respect for their position. As time passes, you'll note that the other person, if they care about you, will try to avoid similar situations, or at least come talk to you about their points of view, without you needing to initiate the conversation.

A relationship isn't like a war, we make it so. Dating and relationships are a high-level negotiation between two people who enjoy each other's company and want to remain beside each other, and so are continuously trying to find common ground to stand on.

In any talks, fights and disagreements that you may have, get rid of the idea of 'win' or 'lose', because there is none. It's just 'lose' and 'lose' all around.

People think and act in a way that reflects the sum total of their life experiences. They have acquired their beliefs and world-views by going through the ups and downs of life, just as you have. If either party feels like their needs, opinions, or points-of-view are being ignored or taken lightly, it leads to bitterness. And nothing kills a good relationship like bitterness.

While having a disagreement, keep your attention on

understanding both sides and trying to find common ground through it. Keep vocally reminding yourself and your partner that you care about each other and that your priority here is to get <u>through</u> the fight, and out to the other side together, rather than to get bogged down by it. It's a lot harder than it sounds, but it's truly worth the effort.

Key Tip #18

Trust Is Imperative

Trust is the most basic thing required for a good relationship. Without it, there is literally nothing left. There are various kinds of trust that come with a strong bond. The trust in having each other's back no matter what, the trust in being faithful and loyal to each other, the trust in caring for what the other wants or being a support through the other's problems. You can trust someone not to rob you when you have your back turned, whilst not trusting them to stay faithful to you. And here's the kicker – you either trust someone or you don't, there's no such thing as 'sorta kinda trust'.

When you want to figure out if you're dating the right kind of person, ask yourself the important 'Trust' questions. You need to move on if they fail these questions because of their own deeds, regardless of how good you might feel with them at the point.

Let me clarify here though – it is not a matter of trust to want someone you're with to say yes and go along with everything you say and believe. People are individuals, and even the best matched couples have some major differences. If you really need never to be disagreed with, what you're looking for isn't a quality partner, but a stuffed animal with no thoughts of his own.

Similarly, any partner who treats you that way has very little intellectual respect for you – you need to talk to them about this right away!

Key Tip #19

Jealousy and Possessiveness vs. Suspicion

Jealousy and possessiveness are very personal, individual traits. Some people feel them very intensely, whereas others barely feel them at all.

They may come from your own emotional issues, past experiences, lack of trust in your partner, or simply your intense feelings towards the person you're with.

It's okay to feel jealous and possessive, but only up to a point, and it depends very strongly on the way you choose to deal with these feelings. If you deal with them in a positive way, I can promise you that your partner may start loving you more for them.

If these feelings come from within you, without any real cause from your partner (and be fair and brutally honest with yourself here), then turn them into a good thing. Be extra affectionate to your partner, but only after you've stepped away from the situation that brought it up. Don't think that being extra clingy during the situation, or acting immaturely and aggressively, will score you any brownie points with the person you're with (and really, that's the only person whose opinion of you matters in this discussion). Instead of trying to mark your territory like an animal during the encounter, use the intensity of your emotions later, in your lovemaking, or whichever other level of intimacy you two may be at by that point.

Whenever these feelings come up, mark your territory by making yourself indispensable to your partner, physically, emotionally or mentally, instead of growling at a threat and risking seeming immature, insecure and juvenile.

However, if you feel like the jealousy and possessiveness is because of insecurity caused by lack of trust in your partner, you need to ask yourself the important 'trust' questions again. Someone who flirts around harmlessly, but whom you know cares about you deeply, will always have your back and will never cheat on you; need not fail these answers. That situation comes down to a difference in world-view and values. You need to have an honest discussion about it with him. Let him know in what way his behavior upsets you, and find a path that works for both of you.

However, there's a major difference between these traits and suspicion. While jealousy and possessiveness may be okay to an extent, undue suspicion is not. You either trust your partner or you don't. If you don't trust your partner because of their own deeds while they were with you, then you need to talk to them about it and move on.

If you do trust them, and you're prone to undue suspicion, you need to remind yourself of all their honest efforts and devotion towards you, whenever you feel this emotion arise. Undue suspicion builds up bitterness on both sides over time and, as I've mentioned before, nothing kills a good relationship faster.

Key Tip #20

Sex Is Not a Weapon!

This is an extremely important point to remember when you're dating or in a relationship. Many partners use sex as a way to enforce their behaviors, tastes and opinions on the people they're with. Be warned that this will only work with weak-willed people. Sex is a way for two people to physically connect and have fun, to enjoy intimacy and comfort, to satisfy and feel satisfied in return. It's not an electric dog collar.

While the power dynamics in many bedrooms swing one way or the other, depending on tastes and proclivities, take care to not let it spill outside your bedroom life.

Be aware that every time you do use it as a tool, what you're also telling your partner is 'Our physical intimacy and sex life mean so little to me that I'm ready to throw it aside every time you disagree with me or have a tiff'. The reason I mentioned that it would only work with weak-willed people is that someone who pushes aside their thoughts or beliefs in order to sleep with you again can't possibly be a strong, equal partner. They're about the equivalent of a dog being coaxed with a piece of salami.

Anyone with self-esteem would be horrified at their desire for you being abused so blatantly, which in turn would damage their attraction towards you, which would ultimately bite your relationship in the rear in a horrendous way. Be aware that I'm not talking about serious fights, disagreements, or breaches of trust here, during all of which sex shouldn't come up as a factor anyway.

Use physical intimacy to reward, if you must, not the lack thereof to enforce or punish.

Key Tip #21

Online Dating - The New Battleground Frontier

Transparency and Honesty are key words here. There are so many men and women turning to online dating as an option to meet the certain someone of their dreams. And while there are many failures, there are resounding successes as well.

I know of a couple that met online, through a game. Though neither of them was looking for a relationship with anyone at the time, and certainly not through this game, they hit it off instantly and soon found themselves falling head-over-heels. They were separated by continents, but they persevered and worked through it all for two years, because each believed that the other person was the right one for them, and they didn't simply want to let this indispensable bond go because of hard work. They were finally able to physically be together only recently, and are now happier than they'd ever been before in their lives, though like any other worthwhile relationship, it still takes work.

When asked about what helped them work through it all, they gave the following pointers:

(a) Get face-to-face as soon as possible, and then make it as regular as possible. Once you've made a connection with someone, either physically meet up as soon as you can, or use video chat software like Skype. Internet cafes everywhere are equipped with web cams to one degree or another, even if you don't have your own, so it shouldn't be too hard if you both really want to make it work. This negates the possibility of you being swindled. If someone seems to be making a lot of excuses here, assume they're hiding something and confront them.

(b) Be as transparent as possible once you've visually confirmed who the person on the other end is. Online dating brings up as much skepticism as it does hope, and the possibility of the person on the other end being a fake is just too strong. Don't start revealing sensitive data right away, or even your exact location, but at least start talking about who you really are and the city you're in. This affords you some protection, while still respecting the biggest key to making this work: Honesty.

(c) Set up regular lines of communication, texts, phone calls, video calls, etc.

(d) Treat it like you would a normal relationship, or date. That means the same level of fun, fidelity, honesty and transparency as you would expect in a normal one.

(e) Figure out what you want out of it and where you want it to go, and talk about it together once some time passes. Knowing what you both want out of your relationship not only helps you to start working on your plans, it also tells you whether you both feel the bond is worth the work. Keep the end result you both want in mind at all times. Unfortunately, 9 out of every 10 of these relationships will not be worth the effort and complication to one person or the other.

(f) Patience. Lots of it. This is going to be even harder to pull off than normal dating, and if the distance is big enough then the stakes are higher too.

(g) Realism vs. Romance of the forbidden fruit: You need to be brutally honest with what appeals to you in the other person. This is going to be a tricky road to navigate, and if self-denial and deception is what's carrying you through it then you will regret the journey's end for the rest of your life. Just like a normal relationship, you need to distinguish between reality and rose-tinted glasses. If you find that it's just the appeal of the forbidden fruit, then you need to break it off for both your sakes.

Conclusion

Never underestimate the power of your instinct (your "Gut Feeling") when it comes to dating and relationships. However, you should also be honest enough with yourself to recognize when something doesn't quite feel right, when you ignore your own instincts because you're awash with hormones, a romantic crush, and a rose-tinted view of the world. Your ideal partner should be able to provide all of it for you, the head-spinning joy of emotions, the heart-pounding rush of hormones, and the thrill of intellectual curiosity, satisfying your heart and your brain.

Exercising the tips in this book should make a difference to how you carry yourself in your dating life and relationships, and improve it significantly by making the obvious pitfalls and mistakes easier to avoid and resolve.

Always remember the three edicts I gave you at the start.

1. Dating is <u>Not</u> a status symbol.

2. Who you d<u>ate</u> says absolutely <u>nothing</u> about

you. You are defined by yourself – your own values, beliefs, and actions – not by who you have on your arm.

3. There is no such thing as an easy relationship, just one that's easy to start. This is especially true of any relationship truly worth having. Whether or not you're willing to work on it is what sets apart a worthy relationship vs. the alternative.

Now get out there and find the partner that you want to flirt with, fight with, make up with, live with, love with, and most importantly grow with. And thanks for reading this book! If you enjoyed it or found it helpful, please take a moment to leave a review on Amazon – that would be much appreciated!

Happy Dating!

Printed in Dunstable, United Kingdom